MONDAY'S TROLL

Poems by
JACK PRELUTSKY

Pictures by
PETER SÍS

GREENWILLOW BOOKS, NEW YORK

The full-color art was reproduced from oil
and gouache paintings on a gesso background.
The text type is Veljovic Bold.

Printed in Singapore by Tien Wah Press
First Edition 10 9 8 7 6 5 4 3 2 1

Library of Congress Cataloging-in-Publication Data

Prelutsky, Jack.
Monday's troll / by Jack Prelutsky ;
pictures by Peter Sís.
p.   cm.
Summary: A collection of seventeen poems about
such unsavory characters as witches, ogres, wizards,
trolls, giants, a yeti, and seven grubby goblins.
ISBN 0-688-09644-1 (trade).   ISBN 0-668-14373-3 (lib. bdg.)
1. Children's poetry, American.   2. Witchcraft—
Juvenile poetry.   3. Wizards—Juvenile poetry.
4. Fairies—Juvenile poetry.   [1. American poetry.
2. Supernatural—Poetry.]   I. Sís, Peter, ill.   II. Title.
PS3566.R36W43   1996   811'.54—dc20
95-7085   CIP   AC

CONTENTS

I TOLD THE WIZARD TO HIS FACE

I told the wizard to his face,
"You're just a fraud, a phony,
A fake, a sham, a charlatan,
Your spells are pure baloney.
Your hogwash couldn't fool
An unsophisticated child—
What do you have to say to that?"
The wizard merely smiled.

"You see, you have no answer,"
I continued, feeling bold.
"You only use illusion
When you turn balloons to gold.
In fact, your poor pathetic act
Is practically a crime—
What do you have to say to *that?*"
He smiled a second time.

I escalated my harangue,
And blared triumphantly,
"Your prestidigitation
Simply can't bamboozle me!"
The wizard smiled a wider smile.
"Piff poff" was all he said—
Since then I've been but two feet tall
And have a hamster's head.

BELLOW

I'm Bellow the ogre,
I rumble and rave.
I'm craggy, volcanic,
My mouth is a cave.
I grumble and thunder
And yammer and fret,
I gobbled a goblin,
My stomach's upset.

I'm Bellow the ogre,
I bluster and boast,
I roasted a troll,
He was perfect on toast.
My manners are grisly,
My temper is hot,
I nibbled a wizard,
My head hurts a lot.

I'm Bellow the ogre,
I smolder and moan,
I carry a cudgel
Of dragon-tail bone.
I swallowed a giant,
He went down like lead—
Bellow the ogre
Is going to bed.

9

I'M ONLY AN APPRENTICE WITCH

I'm only an apprentice witch,
There's much I've left to learn,
Someday I'll be a witch-in-full,
But I must wait my turn.
My nasty brews, though noxious,
Lack a certain wretched smell,
Sometimes my spells don't work at all,
Sometimes they work too well.

I'm only an apprentice witch,
Just seven centuries old,
The elder witches lecture me
To do as I am told.
I strive to grow more hideous,
I'm working on my shriek,
And I've not fully mastered
How to cackle when I speak.

I'm only an apprentice witch
Who's barely learned to fly,
I've been afraid to go too fast,
Or venture far or high.
Just yesterday I stalled my broom,
And crashed into a ditch,
I'm clearly yet unqualified
To be a full-fledged witch.

INVISIBLE WIZARD'S REGRET

I'm in a preposterous pickle,
My prospects appear to be black.
I witlessly made myself vanish,
And now I can't get myself back.

WE'RE SEVEN GRUBBY GOBLINS

We're seven grubby goblins
You never want to meet,
We fail to wash our faces,
Or clean our filthy feet.
Our hands are always dirty,
We have disheveled hair,
We dress in shabby leggings
And tattered underwear.

We're seven gruesome goblins,
Our habits are uncouth,
We pull each other's teeth out,
Then put back every tooth.
We drink iguana gravy,
We chew polluted prunes,
We dance repugnant dances,
We sing unpleasant tunes.

14

We're seven grungy goblins,
Determined to displease,
We never blow our noses,
No matter how we sneeze.
We smell like rotten garlic,
We burp around the clock,
This soon should be apparent,
We're moving to your block.

15

OGREBRAG

A callow knight in armor,
Appropriately brave,
Displayed his lack of wisdom
And charged into my cave.

He challenged me to battle,
In moments it was through.
He made a tasty morsel—
His horse was tasty too.

I'M A CROTCHETY WITCH

I'm a crotchety witch
Living all by myself,
I haven't one crony,
Not ogre nor elf.
No wizard or warlock
Drops by for a stay,
Hobgoblins avoid me—
I like it that way.

My rooms are suffused
With perennial gloom,
I never go out,
I've retired my broom,
I don't even bother
To boil a few brews,
So I'm not to blame
If there's ooze in your shoes.

Today is my birthday,
I baked a stale cake,
Instead of a candle,
I stuck in a snake,
I've turned thirty thousand
three hundred and three,
The snake snuck away—
Happy birthday to me!

I HAVE GOT
A STEAMSHIP ANCHOR

I have got a steamship anchor
And a huge pneumatic drill,
I am borrowing a chain saw
From a local lumber mill.
I am purchasing a tractor,
And a thousand yards of chain,
An enormous block and tackle,
And a forty-story crane.

I've got stacks of bricks and mortar,
And an oversize harpoon,
Massive spools of wire and cable,
And a fifty-foot-long spoon.
There's a monumental lever,
Vats of mucilage and tar,
And a single pair of pliers
That could grip a railroad car.

I have sickles, rakes and shovels,
Rocket launchers, TNT,
And a record-setting toothpick
That I whittled from a tree.
There's a telescoping ladder
That extends into the skies—
I'm a giant's trusted dentist,
And I've learned to improvise.

MONDAY'S TROLL

Monday's troll is mean and rotten,
Tuesday's troll is misbegotten,
Wednesday's troll is extra smelly,
Thursday's has a baggy belly.

Friday's troll is great and grimy,
Saturday's is short and slimy—
But Sunday's troll is crabby, cross,
And full of sour applesauce.

I THOUGHT I SPOTTED BIGFOOT

I thought I spotted Bigfoot
Right behind me in the street,
There was no way I could miss him,
He had two gigantic feet.
He was utterly imposing,
Standing ten feet tall or more,
And was surely no imposter,
Though we'd never met before.

Every inch of him was covered
With a greasy mat of hair,
When I blinked my eyes in wonder,
Bigfoot was no longer there.
Still, I'm certain that I saw him,
He looked ravenous and strong,
But he simply isn't here now,
So I guess that I was wron . . .

BLIZZARD

I'm Blizzard, a wizard
Of wretched endeavor,
My whims are my own,
And I do as I choose.
I trifle with humans
For simple amusement,
I plague them with hiccups
While shrinking their shoes.

I'm Blizzard, a wizard
Of peevish demeanor,
I'm crabby, I'm cranky,
I'm crusty, I'm cross.
A wave of my wand,
You're a tree in a forest,
A blink of my eye,
And you're covered in moss.

I'm Blizzard, a wizard
Of woeful employments,
My methods are many,
My ways are bizarre.
One snap of my fingers,
You're dripping with syrup,
One twitch of my nostrils,
You're slathered with tar.

I'm Blizzard, a wizard
Of hostile intention,
I'll turn you to tallow,
To jelly, to clay—
Your presence annoys me,
You're ever unwelcome,
I'm Blizzard the wizard,
Stay out of my way!

CHITTERCHAT

You may now make my acquaintance,
I am famous Chitterchat,
  My old witch's dear familiar,
  And a venerable cat.
  I am steeped in ancient wisdom,
   Rich in elemental lore,
    Though my witch knows much of witching,
    I'm replete with volumes more.

    I'm no doddering grimalkin
    Mystified by skeins of yarn,
    Or some simple-minded mouser
    Chasing shadows in a barn.
    I'm no skulker in an alley,
    Culling bones for bits of fish,
   And no pampered portly feline
   Lapping from a porcelain dish.

   I've but little time to trifle
   With such stuff as wool and mice,
   For I'm sworn to guide my mistress
   And provide her with advice.
   If my witch omits essentials,
  I discreetly show her how
  To conduct her incantation—
  It takes just the right meow!

FIVE GIANTS

At our planet's icy summit
Looms the Giant of the North,
Ancient glaciers tear asunder
When he stirs and blunders forth.
His incalculable equal
Is the Giant of the East,
Whose least consequential footfall
Chills the boldest savage beast.

Neither holds the least advantage
On the Giant of the South,
Who can house a pride of lions
In the cavern of his mouth.
All are matched in size and power
By the Giant of the West,
Who regards with condescension
The most lofty eagle's nest.

But the being deep in slumber
At the world's volcanic core,
Could between one thumb and finger
Crush and pulverize the four.
Every titan on the surface
Fears the Sleeper in the Flame,
They are doomed if she awakens,
So they dare not say her name.

MOTHER OGRE'S LULLABY

Hush baby ogre, stop raving and rest,
Slumber, sweet savage impossible pest.
Stifle your tantrum, no kicking, don't bite.
Close your red eye . . . baby ogre, good-night.

UNDERFOOT

I'm Underfoot, the least of trolls,
No bigger than a bug,
I socialize with mice and moles,
My neighbor is a slug.
I lounge on toadstools, lurk in mud,
I'm predisposed to bite,
I'm very fierce, my bit of blood
Is liquid anthracite.

I'm Underfoot, immensely strong,
Despite my tiny size,
My yellow mane is dense and long,
I have enormous eyes.
You can't believe a word I say,
I'm treacherous and sly,
I watch my woods both night and day,
And spring on passers-by.

I'm apt to nibble on their toes
Then, inches at a time,
To shinny up beneath their clothes,
And tickle as I climb.
Perhaps they'll even shed a tear
When I tug on their hair,
Be certain that I'm ever near,
I'm Underfoot . . . beware!

A SOLITARY YETI

I'm a solitary yeti,
Traversing frozen plains,
Upon a constant lookout
For dinosaur remains.

I savor them for supper,
I relish them for lunch,
Their flavor is peculiar,
But I adore the crunch.

IF
I WERE NOT
A WIZARD

If I were not a wizard,
With craft unkind and keen,
You wouldn't have to worry
That you might wake up green.
I couldn't, with no fanfare,
And a minimum of fuss,
Transform you into butter
Or a hippopotamus.

If I were not a wizard,
Unwaveringly weird,
You'd not have sprouted antlers
And a fifty-foot-long beard.
I'd lack the talent to transmute
Your breakfast into leaves,
And there would be no butterflies
Residing in your sleeves.

You'd find no fish and melons
Perched atop your feathered head,
Your ears would not be fashioned
Out of jam and gingerbread.
I'd never have transmogrified
Your nose into a yam,
If I were not a wizard—
But then again . . . I am!

JACK PRELUTSKY is one of the most beloved—and frequently anthologized—poets writing today. He has written over thirty books of verse, edited several hugely popular anthologies, and appeared in more schools and libraries than he can count. Among his most popular books are *The Dragons Are Singing Tonight*, *The New Kid on the Block*, and *Something Big Has Been Here*. He and his wife live in the Seattle area.

❖❖❖❖❖❖❖❖

PETER SÍS was born in Czechoslovakia and now lives in New York City with his wife and two children. His drawings appear regularly in *The New York Times Book Review* and other publications. He is the author-artist of *The Three Golden Keys*, *Komodo!*, *Follow the Dream*, and *A Small, Tall Tale from the Far, Far North*. He has illustrated several books by other authors, including Sid Fleischman and George Shannon.